The Village Can't Do It !

...*Because the Village Does Not Exist in America*

Sandra Hayden

A Response to Hillary Clinton a Decade Later &
an Inside Look into America's Public Schools

authorHOUSE®

AuthorHouse™
1663 Liberty Drive
Bloomington, IN 47403
www.authorhouse.com
Phone: 1-800-839-8640

First published by AuthorHouse 3/14/2011

ISBN: 978-1-4567-2462-7 (sc)
ISBN: 978-1-4567-2463-4 (e)

Library of Congress Control Number: 2011900330

Printed in the United States of America

Cover Illustration by Yolanda Presberry
Final Manuscript Editing by Ben Hayden
Draft Manuscript Editing by Nancy Murphy, M.Ed.

"Children Learn What They Live"

If a child lives with criticism,
He learns to condemn.
If a child lives with hostility,
He learns to fight
If a child lives with ridicule,
He learns to be shy.
If a child lives with shame,
He learns to feel guilty.
If a child lives with tolerance,
He learns to be patient.
If a child lives with encouragement,
He learns confidence.
If a child lives with praise,
He learns to appreciate.
If a child lives with fairness,
He learns justice.
If a child lives with security,
He learns to have faith.
If a child lives with approval,
He learns to like himself.
If a child lives with acceptance,
and friendship,
He learns to find love in the world.

Dorothy Law Nolte

DEDICATION

This book is dedicated in part to my Mother, Jane K. Lynch, who inspired me at an early age to be the best I could. The consummate homemaker, Mother taught home economics in public secondary school for thirty years. She also taught me many lessons in life and provided me with an even broader perspective in her ultimate struggle with Parkinson's disease. Her favorite poem, *"Children Learn What They Live"*, by Dorothy Law Nolte, was reproduced in the beginning of the book. It hangs in a frame on the wall of my kitchen. She insisted that children were gifts from God and that they were only granted to us for a temporary time of love and safe keeping. My Mother often cautioned me not to become "a jack of all trades and a master of none" but I did not learn that lesson well. My life has been an endless stream of adventures, experiences and several careers. I have learned much, but as Mother was afraid, I have mastered none. Towards this goal, I still strive. The lessons which I have discovered as a mother and teacher myself, I share with you.

My other dedication is to my husband, Joe, who has given me unwavering love and encouragement throughout our 28 years of marriage. He, like my Mother, has pushed me to be the best that I can be. No matter what my dream or where I wanted to go, Joe was always behind me, urging me on and supporting me. It is because of him that I experienced my greatest joy in life: our son, Ben, who is now twenty-four years old. Ben provided valuable critical feedback on my book drafts and made essential final edits.

FOREWARD

It has now been over a decade since Hillary Rodham Clinton published her book, *It Takes A Village: And Other Lessons Children Teach Us*. At the time of publication, Bill Clinton was President of the United States. I was working as a human resources manager, and had been immersed in a twenty-year career in the business world. Frankly, after successfully climbing the corporate ladder and repeatedly disciplining adults in the workplace, I was burned out. It was in the summer of 1996 when I made my decision to pursue another career with the support and encouragement of my husband and son. Though I already had my bachelor's degree in Political Science, with a minor in Business Administration, I would return to college to pursue a Bachelors and teaching certificate in secondary education. It was only after I had been teaching middle school for six years that I finally read Hillary Clinton's book. Admittedly curious, I was eager to learn how a village could replace a loving, nuclear family unit.

No matter what you think of either her politics or of her personally, most every woman in America would confess to being curious about what makes Hillary Clinton tick. A successful lawyer, mother, First Lady-turned-Senator-Presidential Candidate-Secretary of State, there must be substance to what she had to say. So, color me curious! I checked out *It Takes A Village: And Other Lessons Children Teach Us* from the library for summer reading in 2006.

As I began to peruse the pages, my first impression was that of pleasant surprise. This woman, who seemed cool and aloof in every aspect of her public persona, was seemingly transformed as a very caring and compassionate author who had only the best interests of children at heart. However, as I delved into the book further, I found that I had significant disagreement with some of Mrs. Clinton's conclusions and recommendations for addressing the needs of American children.

Halfway into her book, I began making some notes and considered writing a reply to her viewpoint, utilizing the knowledge I had gained in the public education arena, in general and my school, in particular. Mrs. Clinton inspired me to recount some poignant circumstances and incidents encountered in my classroom. She also challenged me to develop some suggestions to help American children of all socio-economic backgrounds be successful in our society and to realize "The American Dream". Consequently, she helped me reach several conclusions about parenting and education in America. Mrs. Clinton also got me thinking about how all of our American children could be pushed to be the best they can be. However, in actuality, the demands of special education in our classrooms prohibit this hope for most of our low-average children. This book will share some personal and professional insights, as well as some apparent truths which I have come to realize from my experience as a teacher and a mother. Alternatively, with all due respect, the village simply can't do it. Mrs. Clinton was very wrong in her assumption, because the village does not exist in America.

Table of Contents

Introduction

Hillary Clinton and I have much in common by virtue of our age; she is just a few years older. Needless to say, school back in the 1950s and 1960s was significantly different than it is today. Most mothers were true, full-time homemakers, which was a respected career, and now is undervalued. Children were expected to be respectful of adults at all times. When a child who misbehaved in school arrived home, there would be a much worse punishment awaiting them from their parents than they received in the Principal's office. Back then, corporeal punishment was not unheard of in schools. Very few students were poorly behaved. Most of us were always well prepared for school with breakfast in our bellies, homemade lunches, and plenty of pencils with erasers in our book bags. We were afraid not to complete our assignments, since a parent was always looking over our shoulder. Parents played a major role in ensuring that our homework was completed, and there were consequences for failing to turn in things when they were due. Mothers and fathers were diligent in instilling the positive qualities of character and good citizenship.

In those classrooms, rigorous hours of memorization and emphasis on the "Three Rs" were the accepted norms. Reams of paper were consumed outlining sentences and writing rough drafts. There were no computers. Such were the facts of life in my junior and high school years. We also had to pass standardized tests each and every year. If students failed to meet those standards, they were held back in their grade until they achieved mastery of the requisite skills.

Fifty years later, things are very different in the middle school in which I teach. Students are not held back if they had been held back in the previous year or if the students, teachers and administrators believe it would not benefit the student non-academically. If a boy or girl is deemed emotionally immature and thought to need more time for emotional growth, they are sometimes held back. However, if a failing student has displayed habitual disciplinary problems, they are quite often passed on to the next grade. This way, they will be out of the school on schedule in two more years, rather than spending a fourth year in the middle school. With the passage of the "No Child Left Behind" legislation of the George W. Bush era, Congress sought to force public school systems to bring all students to proficiency levels in math and reading by 2014. Many school districts in impoverished rural or center city areas are facing great difficulty in raising their student test scores to show adequate yearly progress towards proficiency of their students.

In my middle school, our special education student population has soared to a whopping 40% in the 2010-2011 school year. That fact in itself puts our school at risk in achieving proficiency, never mind the low socio-economic status of many of our students. For the past two years, we have not met our required scores for annual yearly progress on Maryland Standardized Assessments

(MSAs). We missed the attainment of adequate progress, the measure of whether a school is progressing satisfactorily in just one category: special education students on the 8th grade math test. Sadly, because of only three students' failure, our whole school of 600 students was deemed unsuccessful. This shortcoming is both frightening and disheartening to me and my fellow staff, all of whom are highly-qualified teachers and who put their hearts and souls into educating our youth day in and day out. Unfortunately, this scenario is playing out in many public schools all across America and it has to stop. The shortcomings of this twisted reality should be a huge concern to all citizens of the United States, whether they have children of school age or not. Now, as throughout the history of this great nation, we must recognize that our children are our future, and everyone has a stake in their education.

Where Hillary Clinton envisioned a village to fill the gap created by the current lack of parenting, I have witnessed the absolute lack of a village in America which could bridge this gap. No amount of highly qualified teachers, mentors, character education training, community volunteer programs or exposure to counseling and remediation can replace the fundamental and indispensable role of loving and committed parenting. It was naive on the part of Hillary Clinton to draw analogies of a village to the diverse and industrialized nation that is the United States. It is, indeed, a fact that Mrs. Clinton's village does not exist in America.

Chapter One

Sadly, TheVillage Does Not Exist in America

The term "village" implies a social system where everyone is generally on the same socio-economic level. It invokes a somewhat primitive connotation. A village is a rural area smaller than a town but larger than a hamlet. A village, by its very definition, implies a tightly-knit group of people with very strong bonds and shared cultural norms. In fact, villages are quite small. When examined by outsiders, villagers appear to enjoy many similar cultural characteristics, and possess an often socialistic way of life. This is engrained in their governance and reflected in their economic systems. If we had a village, as Mrs. Clinton implies, the villagers would have a better chance at raising the communal pool of children. However, the characteristics of a village are in stark contrast to the hectic, multi-cultural fabric of the society we know as these United States of America.

Indeed, America today is a patchwork quilt of a very frantic and fragmented humanity. Families more often than not reside in buildings or neighborhoods where they do not know their neighbors. Young people are free to move around the country as never before in our history. Family members and extended families no longer live in the old family neighborhood, let alone in the same state where they were raised. The horizons for American families no longer extend to state and national borders, but beyond and into a "global" village. While not a bad thing, in and of itself, this does prohibit any village-type mentality from developing in the United States. Mrs. Clinton's challenge to all of us to build strong families and communities in order that our children are well cared for and so that our democracy remains strong is a worthy endeavor. Over a decade later, however, America has failed miserably at this challenge.

First of all, it takes a firm foundation of parental and family norms in order to raise children who feel loved, safe, and well grounded. In a village, typically the female is responsible for maintaining the home and caring for children. Daily chores are performed by village women at home: fetching water, cooking, tidying the home – usually only one or two rooms, tending crops and animals, and ensuring sufficient and clean clothing for the family. Village men pursue hunting and various occupations. In our modern America, when two parents are in the picture, they are likely both working outside the home. In a single-parent American household, children are more often than not spending less time with a parent out of the necessity for the single parent to earn a living. In both American home situations, children are carted off to daycare during the workweek, meals are rushed, and quality time at home as a family unit is at a premium.

Research shows that it is in the first year of life when children learn to either trust or to be distrustful. Infants left in their cribs to cry for extended time, as is often the case in daycare situations, tend not to develop a sense of security and trust. Mrs. Clinton mentioned the cutting-edge of this research in her book, when she cited that emotional development occurs primarily between 8 and 18 months of age. The original research by American Eric Erikson, essays of which were published in ***Identity: Youth and Crisis*** in the early 1900s, has been well substantiated by many modern psychologists.

Secondly, in order to have strong communities in the U.S.A. where "villagers" - family, neighbors and friends - truly care for our children there must be grassroots commitment. By commitment, I do not simply mean monetary commitment, although local and state governments in America traditionally provide some basic safety nets for families during periods of hardship. Rather, that in a village, individuals are by virtue of their shared norms, committed to working closely together to care for their children properly, while parents go about their daily work. I teach in a town named Havre de Grace, Maryland. Havre de Grace is nestled on the Susquehanna River, at the head of the Chesapeake Bay. It is approximately 40 miles north of Baltimore. In this community, the senior citizens who frequent the community center are actually afraid of our middle-schoolers. Although they make monetary donations of school supplies each year, they refuse to make a personal commitment to local youth. It is not that they are bad people, but they have heard the stories of our youth becoming disrespectful of authority and elders. They are aware of the rise in crimes that the local "tweens" and teens are committing: petty thefts, breaking community curfew, and vandalism.

As a prelude to my Master's thesis, I began investigating the possibility of developing a partnership with the local senior citizens organization, which is housed in the community center behind my school. When I surveyed them in 2009, not a single person indicated they would be willing to tutor one of our students after school or assist in formal mentoring or in a literacy improvement program with our students during the school day. I was shocked and, needless to say, stunningly disappointed. The town where I teach is not particularly crime-ridden. However, the elderly population has impressions that have been colored by the national news. A community unable or unwilling to impart knowledge and experience its youth is a community that will eventually break down. It is just a matter of time. And, as each year passes, I see that self-fulfilling prophecy being realized.

Thirdly, while not all Americans are earning a living wage, parents must instill in their children the importance of making the most of their public education. This also requires significant effort on their part in helping their sons and daughters maintain that commitment. Many parents do not stress to their children the importance of doing well in school as they enter kindergarten. They must encourage their kids to be the best they can be from infancy; read to them; play educational games with them; inspire their self-confidence. By the time a son or daughter is in high school, it is too late to tell them they need to study in order to do better in school than their parents did. The best chance at a stable career and adequate income in America is for our children to get a good education. If it isn't valued at home from an early age, it will not be valued by children. The American dream is still very much alive and attainable; just look at the many examples in mainstream media, in medicine, business and technology. This does not take into consideration the many thousands of others who have achieved their dreams in pursuit of sports and entertainment. It just takes perseverance, lots of hard work.

Fourth, community leaders must initiate volunteer organizations which conduct adult literacy, tutoring, marriage counseling, and parenting programs. The key word here is *volunteer*. Our government is overburdened with debt and cannot afford to provide these services on a wide-scale basis. Instead, we must incentivize nearby businesses, community colleges and universities to develop strong community partnerships with our school children. This is a sad but true reality when considering the feasibility of relying on Mrs. Clinton's village to raise our American children. Except for our schools or churches rarely do we hear of a person who seems to have time and the inclination to step-up and volunteer to assist our children who are so desperately in need of help outside of their family and school. Local school administrators really need to become proactive in developing partnering programs that have benefits for both the schools and local commerce. This is America's reality.

We cannot expect our government to administer - nor can it afford to fund -all social and safety nets required for the youth of modern America. A corps of volunteers is needed in every community. The federal government is ill equipped to fill these gaps. We desperately need a systematic program of volunteerism. But, realistically, this will never happen in America because of the high-speed pace of our society. There are simply too many unwanted, neglected and disengaged children in the United States who are lost and floundering. Many of them just need a sound role model who will befriend them. Each year, I witness at least five or six of my 100-plus sixth grade students among that despondent group. I am helpless to make it better for each of them. My school's guidance counselors, psychologist, and student services professionals, are overwhelmed by the volume of students they serve. Many parents subscribe to "a village can do it" mentality, and they rely on the school resources to fill the void left by their lack of active parenting. The student services workers make their living trying to create some semblance of the village, which does not exist in America.

The statistics show crimes of abused and/or neglected children predictably manifest in anti-social, and often criminal, behavior. In her book, Mrs. Clinton called for homes, schools, hospitals, businesses and media to do a better job "raising our children even when the odds seem weighted against us". A decade later, we have learned that it is impossible for the government, schools, social agencies, corporations, and the greater community to raise our children for us, as she suggested. If we have learned anything from our public school system, it is that spending more money on education will not better prepare our children. There is no substitute for one-on-one human interaction between children and adults. Many boys and girls crave more opportunities for adult companionship. Failing the capability of a family member to provide these prospects, comprehensive volunteerism programs would help to resolve this need.

Any threads that may be left of a true village in America today are simply too thin and too few. There is clearly no substitute for loving parents and a stable, secure home life. And, sadly, the family unit has become a broken jigsaw. In America, the village can't do it, because a village does not exist. A new flood of immigrants from all over the world arrived on our shores in the last three centuries, each with its own unique culture. The work ethic among the American population in the 19th and 20th centuries was unsurpassed in the world. Our worker productivity was the envy of all industrialized nations. The Civil Rights Movement ended segregation of American schools and opened doors previously closed to African-Americans. Women, whose mothers had worked during World War II out of necessity, found themselves wanting to work out of the home by choice. Many began burning their bras, demanding they be allowed to pursue careers and demonstrating for equal rights with men. Even through all of this, however, we managed somehow to maintain our village. Neighbors went out of their way to help each other, and people made it their business to become involved in positive ways in their communities. So it went in America through the 1950s, and then it began to change.

Bit-by-bit over the next several generations, our country began to evolve into fragmented society. Two-story apartment buildings with five or six families living in them gave way to high-rise apartment complexes with hundreds of residents. Family farms and forested land were sold to developers for large shopping malls and housing developments, where several hundred tract homes were built. The suburbs became the panacea for American life in the 1960s and 1970s.

The post-war era of the 1940s and 1950s gave way to a booming economy, everyone wanting to hold down a job, and many people relocating in order to better themselves. Women realized they could hold down jobs as well as their male counterparts, and they liked the freedom afforded them outside of the home. Large corporations were building new manufacturing plants and began transferring families all over America, and eventually all over the world. At this point, we began the dissolution of the village cohesiveness and the destruction of cultural enclaves in America's towns and cities. Neighborhoods previously dominated by first and second generation Slavic, German, Italian or Irish immigrants became mixed. The cultural ties that had bound those neighbors became unraveled. The village gradually became non-existent.

Chapter Two

Spirituality, Nurturing and Security of America's Children

It is clear that Mrs. Clinton had only the best interests of children in mind when she wrote her book. She made clear the dangers to children in our society, from violence, to neglect, substance abuse, sexual predators, greed and spiritual emptiness. As I get to know the students in my classes each year, I am struck by the spiritual void and lack of depth that the majority of them possess. In fact, it is what I would describe more as a hollowness, lacking empathy, compassion, charity and humility. The void of spirituality in the lives of our children is alarming. In times of crisis, they have few coping mechanisms and nowhere to turn except lashing out – verbally and physically. Couple this with their lack of patience and we are experiencing more bullying and fighting in our schools today. Ultimately, it falls to school guidance counselors or administrators to try to de-escalate situations before they truly turn violent.

Public schools no longer provide courses on philosophy,

reasoning and values, as most early Americans studied. Those types of studies tended to reinforce the values and common sense that was taught at home and helped to preserve a cohesive society. Children were taught a refinement of thought and feeling. Examples throughout history were offered to show youth how choices were weighed and decisions were made. Classic literature provided standards of good character, virtue and courage. Through heroic characters students learned of virtue and selflessness. They were provided with hints on how to navigate their way through delicate situations and how to survive times of adversity. Students were purposefully taught ways to evaluate relationships and diffuse social conflicts without resorting to physical violence. These would be very helpful courses for American youth, from which all of them could benefit. But, there is no time in the curriculum-packed public schools to teach to any end except standardized tests.

In addition to a lack of spirituality in these children, I have found many of their guardians to be disingenuous. They often pay lip service to caring about my students: stepparents, aunts & uncles, grandparents and older siblings who are their primary caregivers. However, in truth, many of these adults do not put their money where their mouths are. Parents routinely fail to show up for their conferences with teachers, and frequently do not call to reschedule. They often make excuses for their poor performing children. Most who should attend evening parent conferences because their children are failing do not take advantage of the opportunity to meet with teachers to gain insight into how they may help.

Additionally, numerous children are simply suffering

from broken hearts by the time they reach me in sixth grade. Broken families are torn to shreds by divorce, pregnancies outside of wedlock, drug and/or alcohol abuse, parental incarcerations and nasty custody battles. Take a closer look around your own town - the plight of uncared for and under-cared-for children is evidenced in every community, no matter rich or poor. Young "tweens" ten to twelve years old stroll the streets at night unsupervised. Several of my students have told me that they do not have to be home until 11:00 p.m., even on school nights. Teachers and school staff try to fill some of the void from lack of care, but it is not possible, nor is it advisable, for us to become overly involved in our students' personal lives.

Unfortunately, Mrs. Clinton was more than a bit unwise in thinking that a village could take the place of a loving, core family unit. Over a decade later, I wish I could say that well-intentioned strangers and social programs have been able to fill the void left by neglectful parenting, but I have many first-hand experiences that prove otherwise. Our youth daily face the challenges of shared custody, having parents in jail for years, being raised by grandparents. and spending time in foster homes. Surely, these realities in childhood are not easily overcome. The scars last a lifetime and, in many instances, lead to some degree of dysfunction in adulthood. Indeed, they sometimes originate a cycle of despair and neglect that repeats itself in subsequent generations.

Unlike the laid-back, slow-paced life in tribal societies, ours is hectic. Adding still another dimension is the extreme violence that exists in America. American society forces a gloomy reality upon many children who are left to fend for themselves. In my first year of teaching I quickly came to realize that teaching was more of a calling than a vocation. Before I embarked on this second career, I had decided that I wanted to give something back. Since my husband and I were blessed with a wonderful son and an abundant life, I wanted to try and pass on some of those same good things to other children, if I could. I, like Hillary Clinton, was naive and optimistic over a decade ago.

However, now I see that America is realizing the effects of what I refer to as second-generation daycare children. Like them, their parents were sent from the home to a place with twenty or so other children, each vying for the attention of only two or three adults for eight to ten hours a day. There they learned to compete with each other for very scarce resources - toys, snacks, one-on-one time with an adult, etc. Aggression is a quickly learned human behavior and yelling until you get what you want is an easily transferable trait from older to younger children.

Children learn early that the squeaky wheel gets the grease - in daycare and at home. I am not, however, inferring that all daycare situations are bad or neglectful. I am saying that many children that I teach are emotionally starved and utilize negative behaviors to get the attention they desperately need. Many exhibit a lack of social skills, have no coping mechanisms for anger and frustration, are emotionally scarred, and have difficulty carrying on a conversation with an adult. Still others claim not to know right from wrong, and use that as an excuse for misbehaving. Currently 40% of my school's population has been specifically diagnosed with some level of attention deficit or behavioral disorder that requires them to receive special education services. My middle school of 600 students has two Guidance counselors whose workloads are overwhelming. Often, they find themselves in need of emotional support from staff and teachers, since their days are filled with sad and heart-breaking situations in which they find themselves feeling helpless to make their circumstances better. Their job is emotionally exhausting and they are drained by the close of each and every school day.

One of the most important insights in Mrs. Clinton's book was her discussion of Dorothy Rich of the Home & School Institute, and the necessity of ""mega-skills": confidence, motivation, effort, perseverance, problem solving that is the foundation for self-respect and ethics." These are all essential skills for successful human development, but we find that the majority of our youth are lacking these traits. In order to address these deficiencies, American schools attempt to motivate and instill a work-ethic, teach self esteem and character education and offer anger management and counseling sessions for students.

Despite these efforts, the public school system is unable to stem the tide. It is clear that children will not learn these important skills unless they are also valued by parents and constantly reinforced at home. Sadly, many parents do not even bother to show up for specifically-scheduled meetings with teachers who have indicated concerns regarding their son or daughter. Simply put, many parents do not care enough about their children to give them the time and attention they need to get a shot at being successful in school, let alone in acquiring their "mega-skills" for life. Over the next few pages, I will describe the personae of several of my sixth grade students, illustrating the absence of proper parenting and the lack of support from their family circumstances.

Here are some specific examples from children I have taught in my classroom. Enter Eddie, who was threatening to hurt himself and on several occasions told my other students that he wanted to die. The students who came to me with those concerns were very upset. I immediately sent them to the guidance counselor. Eddie was from a broken home, living with his mother and spending every other weekend with his father and his new wife. He was unhappy, confided to me that he had no friends, and declared repeatedly that he was not smart. Guidance counseling was not working, as I had referred him to the school counselor on several occasions. Only after getting Eddie into a program of psychological counseling did the threats about hurting himself subside. Eddie is currently attending 7th grade and seems to be holding his own.

There was also Dave, who was living with an alcoholic mother and step-father. He never completed homework, had extreme difficulty completing class work and read on only a second grade level. He was unable to grasp math concepts. At eleven years old, he was incapable of adding, subtracting and multiplying, let alone dividing. When he left my sixth grade homeroom in the spring, he still could not remember what subjects he had for each period, not to mention how classes rotated on different schedules. His appearance was always disheveled and he had the air of a waif or an orphan. I would describe his demeanor as helpless. His lack of skills and refusal to work in school led to a pattern of misbehaving and office referrals. In his discussions with our staff, he confided that there was nothing to eat at home. Indeed, once when he was facing out-of-school suspension, he asked how he was going to eat, since his only meal was his school lunch. He was assigned to in-school, rather than out-of-school suspension with that disclosure. After several suspensions for behavioral issues, and two in-patient psychiatric stays, Dave left to become taught at home at the school district's expense. His home teacher, along with his social worker, made sure there was sufficient food and proper cleanliness on an on-going basis for the remainder of the year. Dave did not return to our school this year.

In the case of Alice, sexual abuse had driven her to the point of trying to commit suicide. I watched her enter sixth grade as a vibrant, intelligent girl, with lots of ideas and full of expression. I watched her slowly deteriorating. By January, her experiences were so painful that she was unable to concentrate on her studies and, subsequently, was placed in an in-patient psychiatric hospital, released and then placed in an alternative educational setting. Children should not have to bear such burdens.

Dawn was a bright girl with the sweetest smile and a long, flowing hair. Her parents' divorce was so bitter and confrontational that she went to live with her grandmother. Slowly, I watched her demeanor change from one of a well-balanced child to an emotional and troubled girl. Despair overtook her and she began a pattern of frequent absences. As a result, she developed learning gaps, did not complete assignments, and her grades began to fail. She had many contentious court appearances, the culmination of which ended in custody being granted to her father. Both Dawn and her grandmother were devastated by the decision. They were separated, and the grandmother was forbidden by court order from seeing Dawn. Depression followed, and Dawn never was able to regain the sparkle and enthusiasm she had in the beginning of the school year. In January, she left our school for a special program run by a group of psychologists and counselors in a neighboring county where her father lived. I often contemplate the ill effects of custody battles and how they affect our children.

Cal is a currently sixth grader who is diagnosed with Attention Deficit Disorder. His biological parents are divorced and, as a result, he spends three nights of the workweek with his grandmother and the other two with his father. On weekends, he goes to stay with his mother. Instead of ensuring that Cal has his book bag and all school materials when he is transported to each of these locations, his mother advised me that often he does not. Therefore, he comes to school without his books, notebooks and homework. Rather than rectifying the problem, this mother continues to use it as an excuse for him not studying for tests and quizzes and not being able to hand in assignments. The problem is that it is obviously the failure of the shared guardians to ensure that Cal has everything he needs before he returns to school. Many of my students' parents are enabling their failure. It is both pitiful and sad.

With each incoming class of sixth graders, the number of students requiring psychiatric and social services grows. By mid-November this year, I have had three students pulled from my classes and enrolled in the Intensive Outpatient Program run by Upper Bay Counseling & Support Services. Many children come to school "shut down" in the morning, due to family situations, sexual abuse, criminal activity in the home, or emotional issues.

Many of our children bear burdens that no ten year olds should have to carry. The seriousness of some situations is such that students are removed from their homes during the school year and sent to foster homes outside of our school district. So much baggage for such small shoulders breeds a generation of emotional nonconformists - unpredictable and underdeveloped, lacking those "mega-skills".

All the idealism and enthusiasm that Mrs. Clinton brought to her book I brought to my career as a teacher. But, try as we may, the school system cannot replace the loving family home environment. We all have families and responsibilities we must attend to at the end of the school day. But, still we wish for a perfect world in which we could take some of our students home with us to nurture and raise. We can see so much potential in them where they cannot believe in themselves. Administration and Guidance staff warn against forging emotionally close bonds with our students.

I know first-hand that a village is absolutely no substitute for caring and involved parents, and that secure and loving families are essential. In the year 2010, a majority of America's children are desperately desirous of both a loving mother and father. But, sadly, we are losing ground in the desperate fight to preserve marriages and family units in this nation. It is clearly obvious that no village exists in America.

Chapter Three

Insights from the Classroom

One of the most poignant quotes in *It Takes A Village* is the one from psychiatrist and writer Robert Coles: "Children who go unheeded are going to turn on the world that neglected them." The aspects of trust that newborns and infants either experience or do not experience will mold their view of the world, as well as their immediate environment. In the classroom, I can tell the type of home from which my students hail. In the first week of school, it is apparent which students come from a home with loving and caring parents – no matter whether a single parent household or that of a couple. I can also spot the children who are starved for attention, do not interact positively with other students, or who literally shut down because of frustration or a negative self-image. It is not surprising that the latter group of children receive the majority of my attention in the classroom.

In the late 1970s, Cornell University Professor Emeritus of Psychology, Uri Bronfenbrenner, performed extensive research on how a child's home environment colors the context in which humans form social relationships, develop attitudes about the world, and interact in various settings. As a result of his essay, "Toward an Experimental Ecology of Human Development", Dr. Bronfenbrenner was instrumental in developing a model for Head Start program. He conducted much research on child development and how these interactions develop negatively or positively. Before his death in 2005, Bronfenbrenner concluded from his years of research and observations that the "disruptive trends in American society produce ever more chaos in the lives of our children...depriving our children of virtues such as honesty, responsibility, integrity and compassion." He viewed this danger as running a close second to the dangers of impoverished and unemployable youth. From my vantage point in the public school system, the desirable character traits we would like to see in our youth are sorely lacking.

Largely contributing to this phenomenon is the lack of stable home lives for our children and the absence of a tight family unit. On average, I would estimate that less than 30% of my students have the same last name as their parent or parents. In many cases, they had family members with two or more different last names – half brother and sisters and step siblings. In a few instances, I have had students confide that they did not know their fathers. The numbers of children from broken homes or blended families has soared in the past ten years. Children are often bounced from parent to parent, grandparent, aunt/uncle, or foster homes for brief periods of time. It is a sin what parents are doing to their children. Parents' instability in their personal relations is negatively affecting not only their children but the future of America. Without the continuity of a stable family life, reinforced values, and the security of a loving and secure home, our children will never feel loved - or learn how to love - from their most valuable role models: their parents.

To make matters worse, according to statistics published in 1999 by the U.S. Census Bureau on their website, slightly less than half of all American children ages 0-5 years old were relegated to daycare facilities that were not in relatives' homes. That statistic is regrettable. In 2003, the Census Bureau published another report showing 37% of children under age five as having "no regular arrangement" for childcare during the workday. This left me wondering if almost 40% of American children are bounced haphazardly between relatives, neighbors or friends, left at home alone, or watched by slightly older siblings. In any case, this means daycare outside of the home without the oversight of a family member is a reality for the vast majority of American children before they enter kindergarten. We will not have the results of the 2010 census for some time. However, it is no wonder that accepted norms of our society and critical character traits necessary for the development of law-abiding citizens are lacking in today's youth. Sadly, a majority of America's children are left with few role models and do not have the advantage of learning valuable life lessons from their parents at a very early age. This does not bode well for our country's future or our ability to maintain shared values essential to a viable democratic republic. Day care facilities cannot replace the care of a loving parent or grandparent, whether male or female.

Before I became pregnant with our son, my husband and I decided we would not have a "daycare child" and that one of us would have to give up their career to stay home with the child. My husband, having a relatively new consulting business, offered to place his career on hold. The decision to have one of us at home to care for our son in our home was the best one we made in our married life, from many standpoints. Ironically, it was at the time when his business had really begun generating income. However, the loss in income and material things was well worth it. The year was 1985, just two years after the popular movie "Mr. Mom" aired. Some people thought we were crazy, others saw it as a bad move, and our parents were uncertain. Joe went back to work part-time jobs when Ben began school, and took a full-time employment when he entered middle school. It paid dividends in the way our son approached his schoolwork and excelled.

In the previously cited works of Professor Bronfenbrenner, he stated that an increased level of alienation, poor behavior in school and violence is due in part to the breakdown of core family values and essential cultural norms over time. Eventually, through their immediate environment and ecological transitions, such as daycare, moving to a new town, or divorce, he concluded that children form their perceptions at a very early age. Indeed, one obvious example of this was evident in a comment made to me in the third day of sixth grade. A little girl told me that her father had thirty-one children, and that he usually stayed until the babies were three years old, then he left the mother. She also added proudly that her mother left her father when she was only one year old. As she spoke nonchalantly of this, I wondered if such irresponsible parenting is widely accepted in America today.

In part, I wondered this because in my third year of

teaching, I noticed one of my male students making a list of names. When I asked him what his list was for, he said "These are my baby-mammas". I figured this meant girls he wanted to have babies with, and I was shocked. Last spring, I learned that this same young man had fathered a child with another one of my students when they were both sophomores in high school. Even more heartbreaking, I discovered that this same student served time in jail for beating up the mother just weeks after she brought the baby home from the hospital.

In a desperate, last-ditch effort to combat such unfortunate situations, public schools have undertaken formal sex education and character education programs. A plethora of programs try to reinforce "The 3 R's: Respect, Responsibility and Doing What's Right". Many Maryland schools have adopted a new "PBIS: Positive Behavior Intervention Support" model. The PBIS program assists teachers in rewarding positive student behavior, while more consistently disciplining negative behavior across the school population. As of this writing, the PBIS program has helped in reducing the number of office referrals made in our middle school. In addition to these character-boosting attempts, there are guidance office services which attempt to assist students on a daily basis. However, the number of students requiring personal guidance services has soared over the past few years. The counselors try to intervene, but many times it is simply too little too late. While extraordinary efforts geared towards introducing character and morals to children are being made in our public education schools, parents hold surprisingly little accountability.

The goal of utilizing America's public school systems

to instill values and norms in our children is both unrealistic and unattainable. Try as we may in our roles as teachers and educators to impose character education programs and behavioral plans, these initiatives are not working. If the things we try to teach them in school are not reinforced at home, our efforts will fail miserably. In homes where such values are reinforced, students have significantly increased success in both the classroom and in personal relationships with other children. The influences outside of school on America's youth are too pervasive and make too profound an impression on them. Our society is fragmented. For that reason, the village does not exist in America.

Chapter Four

Special Education is Running Public Education

In his treatise on fledgling America, French philosopher Alexis de Tocqueville warned of dangers the future would eventually hold for us. His book, *Democracy in America*, cautioned that the social experiment of the United States would experience what he called "tyranny of the minority". This, he advised, would develop because of the eventual power that would be afforded in our society to special interest groups. He cautioned that in an attempt to appease all points of view, America would wind up with exactly the opposite of what was intended by the founding fathers: the lack of majority rule. He envisioned a future America where minority interests would actually command more power than the majority interests. Indeed, I believe this has come to pass in many aspects of American society, not the least of which is public education. But, before we look specifically at this angle, let's consider some underlying truths about our current public education system.

The education field has long been criticized for its

attempts at trying new and innovative techniques that may help children learn. Teachers call this "the flavor of the month". For every successful technique, there are many that have failed miserably. Examples of these over the past 30 years are: not teaching memorization skills, the dependence on the whole-language approach to reading, no more phonetics, not teaching spelling, and a host of "new math" methods. Most have been utilized with no improvement in achievement. Many of my colleagues and I hasten to ask, "What was wrong with the old ways?"

In my middle school, students must write what is called a "BCR", an acronym for Brief Constructed Responses, similar to what we would call a paragraph. BCRs must consist of five to six sentences. They are graded on a scaled rubric. BCRs must be practiced and reinforced in all core subjects – language arts (reading and writing), social studies, science, and math. However, even in language arts classes, teachers are not allowed to grade spelling and punctuation – only the students' thoughts and sentence structure.

This is absurd! No wonder American children are barely literate in many of our public schools. New and supposedly innovative ways to teach are simply not effective in doing the job they were intended to do. The old tried and true methods of teaching reading/writing skills, grammar, and math worked just fine. In the new millennia, we were given the federal government's "No Child Left Behind" mandate, which was a brainstorm of the George W. Bush era. So many schools are unable to meet adequate yearly progress goals (AYP) in basic math and language achievement that all curricula, in every subject, now teach to the tests. Many schools fail simply because they fail to meet mandatory progress goals in student populations that are federally designated areas based on race, special education, and whether or not students receive "free and reduced lunch" in school. When the majority of students are unable to meet proficiency standards, public schools receive an unacceptable rating and are placed in various stages of remediation or taken over for remediation to be turned around. This elaborate process is yet more vivid proof that public schools are miserably failing our children.

I attribute the lack of adequate performance on these high-stakes tests in large part to the reality that special education runs our public schools now. Teachers are given student groupings called inclusion classes. Inclusion is an idea that arose from the writings of Lloyd M. Dunn and others in the 1960s. During that period, Dunn and others determined that children with learning disabilities who were given the opportunity to interact with fully functional children in regular classrooms would learn more and fare better in society. On paper, inclusion sounds great. It appears to meet the tests to provide an "equitable" education for all students, including students with disabilities. It seems to be a panacea for both mentally challenged and disabled children, with no ill effects on the other students in the classroom. The theory is that if specially challenged children are mainstreamed with regular students they will acquire critical social skills they would otherwise lack. In addition, this special population would improve their academic achievement. This would level the playing field for disabled students and be a win-win situation for all concerned.

Introduced on the academic scene in a big way in the

1980s, inclusion began as an experiment in determining whether students with learning disabilities really could be pushed to greater success in the regular classroom setting. One big problem that was not thoroughly thought-out deals with the category of students coded emotionally disturbed. These children are protected under the federal umbrella of special education. They are among the population mainstreamed into inclusion classes. In reality, what happens is that the inclusion classroom of 20-30 students often contains two to three students classified as emotionally disturbed and several with Attention Deficit Disorder. Effectively teaching these varying levels of students becomes virtually impossible from the standpoint of meeting all of the students' needs. Average and low-average students are placed with these special education students who have disabilities ranging from mild mental retardation to totally debilitating physical challenges to severe emotional disturbances. I have even taught students with Aspergers Syndrome, Angel Disease, and Bipolar Disorder in my classroom all at the same time. Even with an Instructional Aide in my classroom for the physically disabled child, it is still very difficult. When some children read on grade level, but others are four years below grade level, it makes for a difficult mix when it comes to teaching.

That is exactly the quandary we have in our public schools today. The grouping of students with special needs in language arts and math is normally more homogeneous. However, in all other subjects, inclusion determines classroom composition. This impacts the ability teachers to push their low-average students to become average and proficient students in their subject areas. The very wide range of reading levels of students in inclusion classrooms is astounding. I have taught students in a single classroom who include second grade through seventh grade reading levels. Talk about a juggling act!

Dealing with challenges in reading and comprehension variances, teachers find themselves having to split classes up into smaller study groups or differentiated learning groups. Some special education students in my low-average classes have writing accommodations. This means that they must have a scribe for class notes, on quizzes, and standardized tests. In a class of 20-30 students, having to stop and write notes for one student has an unavoidable affect on the attention spans of the other students. The remaining students become restless and impatient while waiting, which can lead to inattentiveness and potential for misbehaving. I recently had my sole Instructional Aide pulled from my two inclusion classrooms. I have five students in both of those classes that require a scribe for tests, so that gives you an indication of how well they are able to keep up with the pace of daily instruction in my classroom. However, my I.A. was pulled from my classes to become the personal aide for a student in our self-contained, "resource" special education classroom. This student communicates in math problems with blocks and points to pictures when he is quizzed on word recognition. The potential for maximum achievement by my ten low-average students is literally sacrificed for the needs of one child who, as sad as it is, will never be a fully functioning adult in our society. My school is actually not the proper educational setting for such severely mentally challenged children. However, this is a decision that is made solely at the Board of Education level, and we are bound to do the best we can with the resources we are given.

As another example of this, I share my experience this past school year where I actually had a social studies class of 25 students that included one student coded "mildly retarded", two coded "emotionally disturbed", four with Attention Deficit Disorder, and three who read on a third grade level. A special education teacher was assigned to my class. None of these students had an aide to assist them, and at least one day a week I was flying solo - without the special educator in my room. The frustrations that I encountered trying to scribe for three of these children throughout each lesson, while managing to keep the other students actively engaged in class work was a huge personal and professional challenge. Even more painful was administering my eight unit tests to this inclusion class. Nine – yes, nine - of the twenty-five students had unit test accommodations requiring a scribe for their essay questions. This created an untenable situation for each of the eight units in my curriculum, as the unit tests took a minimum of two and in some cases, three full class periods. At the end of every unit test week, I felt as if I had literally been put through a wringer and was left reflecting on my perceived failure for some of these children.

This year I am teaching a very challenging youngster whom I will call Jacob. He came to us coded as having Attention Deficit Disorder and being emotionally disturbed. As such, he has a 504 Plan that legally requires some accommodations be made to his learning environment. Jacob came to us with strict instructions on his behavior plan from his elementary feeder school. If he is having a good day, he will tell you he feels "green". When he feels "yellow" the teacher must watch him for signs of anger and frustration. If he tells a teacher that he is feeling "red", they are to send him immediately to Guidance. There, he is given a jar of pasta and allowed to play with the pasta for 20 minutes, all the while missing class. Only after 20 minutes have passed may he be asked to discuss his situation with the counselor. Once, the counselor was on her way to meet with a parent. He demanded to meet with her instead, and said to her, "When I tell you I am depressed, you have to talk to me." It seemed as if he was challenging her.

Jacob is reading on grade level, can perform higher-level problem solving and is very articulate. However, he rebuffs authority and exhibits what I consider classic symptoms of defiance disorder. He frequently refuses to complete in-class assignments and frequently initiates disagreements with his peers. When I managed to get an Inclusion Helper (IH) for a student in Jacob's class who suffers from a degenerative disease that impairs writing, Jacob complained that he can't write and that he needs someone to scribe for him. I believe he has a learned manipulative personality. Other teachers share my evaluation. As a mother I wonder how a ten year old could be immersed in so much negativity. What in his rearing would cause him to reject reasonable suggestions as some sort of personal attack. As an educator I must contemplate whether or not the majority of his problem stems from simply not getting his own way.

Almost every suggestion an adult makes to help him improve himself is rebuffed in an outright argument by him. The valuable time invested in coaxing Jacob is extraordinary. A case in point is his refusal to attend

Notebook Organization Club, held during homeroom. Our team of teachers recommended several students for the club, since they are unable to keep their binders and notebooks organized. When I insisted for a third time that he attend, I had to walk him into the hallway. He copped an attitude, argued with me and said, "You can't tell me what to do." Eventually he sauntered down the hallway. Within a few minutes of his departure, the phone in my classroom rang. It was the Notebook Club advisor, who said she was sending him back to homeroom since he refused to participate. She said that he was rude and disrespectful to her and that he would not be allowed to come back to the club. I requested a parent conference with his team of teachers. The school year is still new, and I am reserving my final opinion for later.

In Mrs. Clinton's book on raising children, she failed to address the issue of the special needs populations, but they are unmistakably the focal point of our American education system. In many countries, students with special needs are educated separately and apart from other children out of a practical societal need. These special children are taught one craft or skill from a very early age which they can perform for life. But, America is mainstreaming the majority of its special education population into inclusion classrooms. As a result, a large majority of America's average and slightly-below-average students are not being educated to their fullest capabilities. I am not saying that all special education children should be in special classrooms. Many are mentally capable, even though their bodies do not function properly, and they belong in regular classroom settings. However, there are many emotionally disturbed and mentally challenged children who require very small classroom settings with highly specialized attention.

America is falling behind other nations in large part because of the failure of its public school systems to realistically educate special education students. In inclusion classrooms, low-average students rarely have the opportunity to excel to their full capacity, because the weight of the special needs children is pulling them down, out of necessity. Teachers are forced to re-teach concepts in many instances. We are forced to read materials more slowly, we must repeat information more frequently, deal with limited vocabulary in many cases, and move sluggishly through our curriculum. It is true that special needs students do acquire more heightened social skills, but they do so at the expense of the academic achievement of their average and high-average counterparts.

From whatever point of view you analyze it, inclusion classes are encouraging mediocrity in our average students. Those average students who could be induced to excel to above average are not given the opportunities to do so for reasons of disruption, lack of time, and the need for re-teaching to the special education students. We are doing this unconsciously, without meaning to, and without even recognizing it.

I cannot tell you how many times I have wished that I could remove several promising, barely below proficient students from my inclusion classes. We can't remove several students at a time, but we do, often move a single student who is a high performer. Often, placing them in a different academic environment, they are able to master proficiency. With just a little more individual attention and more teacher-centered time, I feel certain I could have made a difference. However, in their inclusion class setting, my time is consumed with trying to bring the special education students to some minimal level of comprehension.

Another reason special education has brought anxiety to the inclusion classroom is the sheer number of behavioral incidents that occur spontaneously, without warning, which must be handled. Do not get me wrong; there are plenty of disciplinary issues that result from the "average" child. That, in and of itself, is the topic of another whole book. However, the number of incidents and the number, nature and the severity of the disruptions from special needs students is real cause for concern. Some make noises that are uncontrollable. Others throw temper tantrums or have been given the right to stand and/or walk around the classroom in their Individualized Education Plan (IEP).

Many are aggressive and have no coping skills when they are frustrated, and this manifests itself in physically harming others. Still others scream and run out of the classroom when, in the simplest of situations, they do not get their way. After outbursts in the classroom, it takes time to explain to the students they need to be patient and calm when these situations occur. All of this, of course, causes loss of valuable instructional time for all concerned. However, teachers are expected to make many accommodations for such students through the use of their IEP.

Now, due to the severity of their disability, some special education students who are disruptive have an aide assigned solely to them throughout the whole school day. However, I have taught several students over the years who have no aide at all and receive services from special education teachers on a hit-or-miss basis. The requirements for these students to receive special education services are based on an hourly basis. More often than not these services are only provided in the tested core areas of language arts and math. The aides in my school frequently have difficulty controlling the students to whom they are assigned when they become unreasonable or physically violent in the classroom. Sometimes, simply not getting their way will trigger a reaction in emotionally disturbed children. In such cases, administrators are called to the room to remove them or the School Resource Officer, who is a member of the local police department, is called to the school.

The traditional public school has difficulty coping with this population, since they are prohibited from disciplining many of these students if their behaviors are a manifestation of their disability. In other words, if the disability contributed to their misbehavior, they may not be punished for their negative behaviors in school. Still others are diagnosed with Bi-Polar Disorder or fall on the Autism Spectrum. Teachers are frustrated and disheartened by the undue and unreasonable pressures of special education.

On a daily basis, parents and families have their hands full dealing with these children at home. Many of these children should not be mainstreamed in the classroom because of the extremely disruptive nature of their behaviors. However, parents fight attempts to place their children in self-contained classrooms or in special education resource classes where they would receive more individualized attention. In addition to being medicated, some children are severely disabled to the point where they are still in diapers and can marginally communicate with school staff. These children require being "bathroomed" by the school nurse throughout the day. Due to such occurrences, some parents refuse to have their children develop a stigma of having to be segregated from the mainstream population. There needs to be some interim classroom between these severely disabled children and the moderately disabled.

The sad fact is that the public schools cannot effectively manage the education of many special ed children utilizing the current inclusion experiment in the classroom, and we are doing a disservice to the low average and average students who are placed in those inclusion classes. The positive effects of socialization for this minority, special population can never outweigh the negative effects that inclusion classes have on the achievement of many low average students. Although well-intentioned, the inclusion classroom is maintained at the expense of the majority of low-average student body. A village would never sacrifice the good of the many for the advantage of the few.

Chapter Five

School Has Become "Uncool"

When Hillary Clinton and I were in junior high and high school, times in America were very different. Our parents had lived through World War II and were used to making do with less; this lesson they tried to teach us. We learned from them that hard work equates to success. Their work ethic was engrained in us. Whether tackling school work or work for pay, if we began a task it was to be pursued to finish, and we were expected to give it our all. We were encouraged to be the best we could be.

At that time, America's fledgling space program was screaming for youngsters to become scientists, mathematicians, and engineers. New discoveries in medicine spurred many of us to become chemists, nurses and doctors. Public schools were homogeneously grouped, and most children of above-average intelligence were expected to attend universities. College education was valued more than ever in a society that had become thrust into the limelight as the preeminent world leader. However, many best and brightest talents of the 1960s and early 1970s were called to fight the war in Vietnam.

College deferments for male students were granted; but once they graduated, our young men were fair game for the U.S. military draft. For us, it was cool to be in school; and, the longer the better for males. And, through it all, our parents believed in us and the productive citizens we could become.

Back then, parents and schools alike expected that children would be successful and that each of us had the potential to live The American Dream. The possibility of failure was rarely considered. Today, however, our public education system seems to be running on the totally opposite premise. We seem to be expecting failure, so we strive to push for some measure of proficiency for all. But, in our mania to move every single student to a minimal proficiency level we are, ironically, achieving mediocrity. Neither our top students nor our below average students are served well. Our average students never become pushed to their personal best. Many special-education and disadvantaged students can, hopefully, attain some measure of sub-proficiency but will be ill prepared for the work world. As a whole, our student body makes moderate attempts at achievement. We rarely encounter students who truly work to their full potential and excel in their studies; we may see six or eight each year. Even the students with the most promise require prodding and are too often satisfied with a grade of B or C, instead of the A that their teacher knows they could achieve with a little more effort.

However, in Hillary's and my experience, we were fortunate to have loving parents who believed in us and helped us become successful. Today's children in many cases do not have this advantage. Rather than see what their children could become and push them towards their goals, parents often tend to make excuses for their child's lack of motivation. Adding insult to injury, basic courtesies and respect are missing from what used to be the fundamental manners of our nation's children. Students slump down in their chairs during teacher conferences and are not confronted by their parents to be respectful and sit up straight. Parents tolerate their children talking back to them, and in some cases parents have told us that they can't control their son or daughter. Therefore, teachers often bear the brunt of disrespectful remarks and cuss words in the classroom.

I have heard more excuses for students from parents in my teaching career than I heard in my career in human resources, when I was dealing with adults and their shortcomings. And, I don't mean excuses that children themselves fabricate. Surprisingly, these are excuses which parents honestly believe to be legitimate. For instance, they will e-mail telling me that homework cannot be completed because there was sports practice last night. Their child was at "the other parent's house" last night, and left their back pack at home, etc. Their son slept over at a friend's house and required another night to study for a test. Their daughter left her project on the kitchen table in the mother's haste to drop her off at school before going to work. The mother's explanation becomes the child's excuse. We have heard every excuse imaginable! Rarely do parents accept responsibility for setting up such scenarios that cause their child's failure. However, they are quite often a large part of the problem.

The bottom line is that many parents, as well as many students, now believe that school is not cool. How many times have I heard "Well, I was never good in school, so that's probably why he isn't good in school." I want to scream, "No! That's not the reason, and why are you coloring your child with failure just because of your own poor work habits or shortcomings?" So many of my students' parents have been enabling their children with excuses for why they are not performing to their potential. It's almost as if they, too, expect mediocrity and are unmotivated to instill in their child a desire for success in their educational endeavors. When children believe their parents don't expect them to succeed, they are pre-disposed to be doomed to failure. Public education is taken forgranted in our United States.

When I was a child, school was of essential importance. Our culture valued intelligent, motivated students. Other children looked up to their high-achieving peers. Now, high-achieving children are often put down, teased and bullied in our public schools. A loss of faith in our children is a tragic loss for the American village that we once had for several centuries. The prospect of a generation of our children being disheartened with school by age 10 and saddled with the failure of their parents before they even have a decent chance at success is untenable. The lessons taught in early childhood begin to construct the framework for a young man's or young lady's self-image. If their shortcomings in school are considered suitable and accepted at home, will some children never be able to believe in the possibilities they might dream for themselves? How very sad a statement on our most basic societal core: the family. When the family unit is no longer fulfilling its primary role in the raising of its children, the village can no longer exist. This is the current status of America's culture.

Now, couple this reality with the bombardment of influences from pop culture and the entertainment media. The result is that we have given rise to a nation of youth who are disrespectful, unmotivated, and self-absorbed. They are only actively engaged when involved in endeavors which interest them. They have difficulty recognizing what they must do, and insist on doing only what they want to do. Discipline is sorely lacking from their family and parents. Therefore, if they are not interested in school, they will do everything in their power to resist doing the work in the classroom, as well as out of the classroom.

On the other hand, these 10-11 year olds are captivated by personal relationships and integrally involved with social networking. This past school year, we had a situation where sixth grade girls were texting each other one evening trying to engage others in the attack of a female student at school the next day. The capacity of our children to invoke such malicious and hateful actions continues to astound me and my fellow educators. This kind of thing happens in high schools, but in our little middle school? Yes. These types of situations occur only in cities, not in our little suburban town, right? Wrong. I actually confiscated eight cell phones from students in my classroom last year. They are forbidden to have cell phones with them in classes and must leave them, turned off, in their lockers.

Each year, the erosion of our youth's character becomes more apparent and more disturbing. The breakdown of our culture is more pervasive year after year, and the gradual deterioration of our country's moral fabric continues to erode. America is devoid of any village. A majority of our children are insecure. They lack academic, emotional coping, and social skills. Our children are in crisis and the future of the America I have known during my lifetime is in danger.

Chapter Six

America's Future Without the Village

There is no denying that the future of America rests solely on the success of all of our children, regardless of their abilities and their challenges. We must do a better job in public education to ensure that all of them can be the best they can be. However, there are many obstacles to this both inside and outside the school building. Without the village to rely on, our broken families and fragmented culture have left many of our youth feeling hopeless, with a negative view of their future. Why were the youth of the 1950s and 1960s so eager to acquire an education, but most of today's youth possess complacency and lack a sincere desire for learning?

Motivating our students to want to learn our curriculum is a full-time concern of teachers. We try to find new ways to connect their learning with prior knowledge in order to increase their understanding of materials. The sad truth is that proficiency is becoming more difficult since the majority have very little prior knowledge. Most have spent little time with adults and have been exposed to only a fraction of the facts about history, language arts and social sciences that we had acquired at their age. However, their awareness of social relationships, sex and drugs is exponential when compared to knowledge sixth graders had about such things when I was growing up. Ten year olds have become the new fifteen year olds, and we can thank the media, music videos, television and video games for this unprecedented awareness. At this age, children should be curious, physically active and desirous of learning. Instead, we find ourselves with children who are content in playing computer games, watching TV or videos all day long. Few seem to even want to play outside for any extended period of time, except for efforts spent in organized sports.

In the absence of the quasi-village in which Hillary Clinton and I grew up, we need to embark on a serious journey for reform of our public education system. We need American children to be excited about school again and to begin believing in themselves and their potential. The greatest force for this realization must be generated by the parents. They need to be positive about school and train their sons and daughters by example, being good role models, reading regularly to their children, and developing a positive self image with encouragement and the security of a loving home. They must encourage their children to begin setting goals for themselves.

I propose moving sixth grade back into elementary schools and reforming middle schools to include the seventh, eighth, and ninth grades. Even more radical is my suggestion for a comprehensive privatization of the primary grades, first through sixth, on a permanent basis. However, private schools - and parochial schools specifically – do have an excellent track record for teaching the basics and setting students on a firm path to character education and good behavior. By the time children reach middle school, they would be able to read, write a simple essay, and perform some advanced math calculations. Local school districts would bid contracts with private and parochial schools that have good track records for both administration and instruction.

Tenured teachers employed in the public school primary grades would be automatically transferred to the private system with comparable salaries and benefits, and as many of the effective administrators as necessary who are currently employed in school districts could be hired by the private system. Although, I must say that I believe most school districts are top-heavy in their central office staffing. These changes would take some pressure off of local schools that experience substandard student performance and have poorly run school districts. School board administration in all districts would by necessity become less top heavy, which is often one of the most troubling ironies in the realm of funding public education. Funding would still be provided by state and local tax revenues, with full curriculum discretion. Private school facilities could be rented by the public system, which could save on capital expenditures for new school buildings. More resources could be freed up to allow for smaller schools and class sizes, both of which would manifest huge improvements in the proper education of America's children. Underprivileged students in poverty-stricken schools would have opportunities never before dreamed and of which they had previously been denied.

We must also introduce more and newer technology in the classroom. And, once in place, make sure that if the technology breaks it is repaired in a timely order. When a work order is placed for repair of a unit, make sure it gets prompt attention. I have waited up to three weeks to have my LCD projector repaired. Technology is great, but when it can't be relied upon to work because tech services fail to make repairs for weeks, technology in the classroom absolutely stinks. Several teachers I work with currently have an LCD projector or SMARTboard which they reported as not working. They often express frustration over the time it takes to get repairs and state they wish they didn't even have the equipment in their room. Once you begin to rely on it, it is very difficult to go back to overhead transparencies and the chalkboard while waiting for repairs.

Another recommendation is for tight, homogeneous grouping of students in all grades. Once public school students get to high school, they can take advantage of Advanced Placement (A.P.) courses, which count for both high school graduation and college credit. Our best and our brightest students are able to take advantage of this wonderful opportunity. However, the mid-average student rarely has the chance to take AP courses, since they have never been pushed to their full potential. They have been muddling through general education courses, mixed with low-average students, and are often under-motivated. If they had been given the opportunity for placement in classes that made them stretch for achievement throughout their elementary and middle school experiences, many of them could realize much greater achievement. These kids are the ones in whom teachers often see as having much potential, but they are absorbed in lethargy. Rather than have two or three ability levels in each grade, there should be five homogeneous levels. As many children who are in the third and fourth tiers should be pushed upward as possible.

With regard to special education, there must be some intermediate classroom option available between the traditional self-contained classroom for severely disabled and mentally retarded - which is a legitimate medical and educational determination - and current inclusion classes. An alternative classroom for the mildly retarded and emotionally disturbed students should be developed separate and apart from low-average students. This would give the low-average students the greatest possible shot at their personal best, rather than becoming turned off by their educational setting.

I truly hope that this suggestion is not viewed as insensitive. I feel strongly about all of our children reaching their full potential – and beyond, if possible. However, the playing field is never totally level and all things in life are not always fair. This is as true in the area of education as it is in all of society. In our zeal to make everyone in America equal, we experience many of our youth falling between the cracks. They will never be able to be successful in the inclusion classroom but yet they are not low enough to be in the self-contained classroom. These children deserve something more, but most public schools do not have alternatives to offer.

In conjunction with homogeneous groupings, the American education system needs to greatly expand the vocational and technical educational opportunities for our youth. These opportunities should be in place to begin vocational, business, service industries and trades exploration in middle grades. Intense, specialized training should be aligned with the major trades of electrical, mechanicals, plumbing and construction, as well as preparation for office, retail, restaurant and hotel careers. These are typically the areas in our economy that employ the greatest number of people. Students should have a good deal of input as they move through their years of self-selection education. Similarly, we must begin to channel special education students into job training tracks and begin basic training for those tracks in seventh grade. This will give them several years to learn, practice and perfect repetitive jobs that will afford them the chance to become independent, self- sufficient adults. Some students will never be able to live as totally independent adults, but we can prepare them for life in group homes, where they are closely supervised and protected as adults.

Clearly, comprehensive school reform is necessary, beginning with the repeal of the "No Child Left Behind" initiative. The federal government mandated this program, but it failed to provide funding to adequately address the comprehensive needs of individual school districts. Unreasonable quotas for special race and low income categories, even when just a very few number of students comprise those categories, were assigned to adequate yearly progress. In the case of many special education students, they will never be capable of securing sufficient progress to meet proficiency standards. Each state was left to determine how it would assess itself.

Only two years ago did my school district commence modified state assessments in math and reading for our lowest achieving special education population. These exams are for lower achieving special education students, but who are still on a diploma track for high school graduation. For several years, we have had alternative state assessments for other special education students who fall in the lowest tier of learners. These are students who are not on the diploma track, but will instead receive a certificate of attendance through twelfth grade. Despite these specialized standardized tests, some of our students are still unable to hold a pencil, or simply cannot write, and have other challenges which require a scribe for all testing. This puts an added strain on schools with a high population of special education students. We need to do away with this ridiculously burdensome and expensive way to assess public education for low achieving students in America. We need one battery of tests that becomes the national standard by which all student achievement is assessed for graduation in every state in the United States. Other forms of assessment should be designed for the lowest achievers.

Lastly, we need a comprehensive system of national teacher certification; no more individual state requirements for Praxis exam scores. We have as many varying standards for making the determination of "qualified" teachers as we do states in the United States of America. That is ludicrous, when you think of the number of teachers, as well as students, who move around the country from state to state. Requirements should be uniform for all students and, likewise, for all teachers.

Instituting these innovations, I can conceive of an American public education system that can once again get on the track to producing the best and the brightest youth in the world. Students will be afforded both more and better opportunities for proficiency and mastery. With feelings of academic success and improved self-image, no child would be left behind. All American children will be able to revitalize their interest in education. Additionally, they will possess pride of ownership in their own education, whether headed for higher education, vocational trades or service industry occupations.

Our vision for America's youth should be of a country where all who are able can be employed, while those who are unable to work are cared for by families and requisite social service programs. The goal of American society should be a multi-cultural nation comprised of parents who love and take full responsibility for their children. Fathers and mothers must both give their sons and daughters the love and security that is essential for positive self image and a feeling that their parents are not just believing in them, but also counting on them to do their personal best. Our children are floundering and they desperately need a lifesaver.

The United States of America is not a village, but a proud nation of individual achievement from personal dreams manifesting in honest, hard work. It is a colorful patchwork quilt of many races, creeds, nationalities and talents. We were built by strong men and women who believed in taking care of their own, not depending on a non-existent village to raise their children for them. Happily, the village does not exist in the United States. If it had, America would neither have been able to achieve its greatness nor become the leader of the free world. The village cannot raise our children for us. The village cannot instill values not at home. The village cannot inspire spirituality in its youth. The village cannot implant moral character in our sons and daughters when their parents have failed. The village does not exist in America.

EPILOGUE

Now that *Waiting for 'Superman': How We Can Save America's Failing Schools*, by Participant Media and Karl Weber, has come to the foreground of America's consciousness, I am hopeful that significant discussion on educational reforms will begin. Those of us in education who saw some media peeks into "Education Nation" did not hold much hope that any meaningful reforms would result. The more insight the American public has into its education system, the better equipped they will be in supporting the necessary transformation. In the process of writing this book over the past three years, I have been waiting for a "Superman" – or "Superwoman" - to enter the scene and undertake the sweeping transformation our American education system needs. This challenge will take a "super-person" to lead the national reforms and thousands of super-individuals to accomplish the extensive innovations required on the state and local levels.

Since we have no village, we will continue to rely on our old-fashioned, tried-and-true Yankee ingenuity. Our boundless American spirit and relentless work ethic will see us through this very challenging and demanding time of educational reform. We all need to believe in the great nation we have become, as well as the great nation that we will continue to be in the future. Our strength is in that belief and in our collective acknowledgement that our children are that future.

REFERENCES

Bronfenbrenner, Urie, Cornell University, "Toward an Experimental Ecology of Human Development", American Psychologist, July, 1977, pages 513-529.

Clinton, Hillary, *It Takes A Village: And Other Lessons Children Teach Us*, Simon & Schuster, September, 1996.

de Tocqueville, Alexis, *Democracy in America*, translated by Arthur Goldhammer, Library of America, 1ˢᵗ Edition, February, 2004.

Erikson, Erik H., Identify: Youth and Crisis, W.W. Norton & Company, Inc., New York, NY, 1968, reissued as a Norton paperback, 1994.

Lang, Susan S., Cornell University News Service, September 26, 2005, http://www.news.cornell.edu/stories/Sept05/ Bronfenbrenner.ssl.html, pages 1-4.

Nolte, Dorothy Law, "Children Learn What They Live", 1954.

Participant Media and Karl Weber, *Waiting for 'Superman': How We Can Save America's Failing Schools*

Rich, Dorothy, *Megaskills: The Stuff Achievement is Made of*, Houghton Mifflin Co., 1988.

U.S. Census Bureau *Survey of Income and Program Participation, "Who's Minding theKids?" Childcare Arrangements, Spring, 2005*, published 2/28/08, http://www.census.gov./prod/2010pubs/ pages 70-121.